AF200062

Impressum
Verlag: BABADADA GmbH, Nedderfeld 112 , 22529 Hamburg
Geschäftsführer / Verlagsleitung: Harald Hof
Druck: Books on Demand GmbH, In de Tarpen 42, 22848 Norderstedt

Imprint
Publisher: BABADADA GmbH, Nedderfeld 112 , 22529 Hamburg, Germany
Managing Director / Publishing direction: Harald Hof
Print: Books on Demand GmbH, In de Tarpen 42, 22848 Norderstedt

classroom
silid-aralan

divide
bawasin

186/2

board
pisara

school yard
bakuran ng paaralan

teacher
guro

paper
papel

write
sumulat

pen
pen

desk
mesa

ruler
ruler

book
aklat

pupil
mag-aaral

satchel

satchel

pencil case

lalagyan ng lapis

pencil

lapis

pencil sharpener

pantasa

rubber

goma

drawing pad

drowing pad

drawing

drowing

paintbrush

pinsel na pampinta

paint box

kahon ng pinta

scissors

gunting

glue

pandikit

exercise book

aklat para sa pagsasanay

homework

takdang-aralin

number

numero

add

dagdagan

subtract

bawasin

multiply

paramihin

calculate

kalkulahin

letter

liham

alphabet

alpabeto

word

salita

text

teksto

read

basahin

chalk

yeso

lesson

leksyon

register

rehistro

exam

eksaminasyon

certificate

sertipiko

school uniform

uniporme sa paaralan

education

edukasyon

encyclopedia

encyclopedia

university

unibersidad

microscope

mikroskopyo

map

mapa

waste-paper basket

basurahan ng papel

hotel
hotel

Grand

hostel
hostel

bureau de change
tanggapan ng palitan ng pera

ROOMS

EXCHANGE

car
kotse

language
wika

yes / no
oo / hindi

Okay
Okey

hello
kumusta

translator
tagapagsalin

Thank you
Salamat

how much is…?

magkano ang…?

I do not understand

Hindi ko maintindihan

problem

problema

Good evening!

Magandang gabi!

Good morning!

Magandang umaga!

Good night!

Magandang gabi!

bye bye

paalam

direction

direksyon

luggage

bahage

bag

bag

backpack

napsak

guest

panauhin

room

silid

sleeping bag

sakong tulugan

tent

tolda

tourist information
....
impormasyon ng turista

beach
....
dalampasigan

credit card
....
credit card

breakfast
....
almusal

lunch
....
tanghalian

dinner
....
hapunan

ticket
....
tiket

lift
....
elebeytor

stamp
....
selyo

border
....
hangganan

customs
....
adwana

embassy
....
embahada

visa
....
visa

passport
....
pasaporte

aeroplane
eruplano

ship
barko

fire engine
bomba

truck
trak

bus
bus

motorboat
banggang demotor

bike
bisikleta

car
kotse

ferry

lantsang pantawid

boat

bangka

motorbike

motorsiklo

police car

sasakyan ng pulis

racing car

kotseng pangkarera

rental car

nirerentahang kotse

car sharing
car sharing

breakdown truck
trak na panghila

refuse truck
trak na pantapon ng basura

motor
motor

fuel
panggatong

petrol station
gasolinahan

traffic sign
karatula ng trapiko

traffic
trapiko

traffic jam
masikip na trapiko

car park
paradahan ng kotse

train station
estasyon ng tren

tracks
riles

train
tren

tram
trambya

carriage
wagon

helicopter

helikopter

airport

paliparan

tower

tore

passenger

pasahero

container

sisidlan

carton

karton

cart

kariton

basket

basket

take off / land

umalis / lumapag

city

lungsod

village

nayon

city centre

sentro ng lungsod

house

bahay

cinema
sinehan

advert
mag-anunsiyo

street lamp
ilaw sa kalsada

street
kalsada

taxi
taksi

snack shop
tindahan ng miryenda

pedestrian
taong naglalakad

pavement
aspalto

zebra crossing
pedestrian lane

bin
bin

crossing
liwasan

traffic lights
mga ilaw trapiko

hut
....
kubo

flat
....
patag

train station
....
estasyon ng tren

town hall
....
munisipyo

museum
....
museo

school
....
paaralan

university

unibersidad

bank

bangko

hospital

ospital

hotel

hotel

pharmacy

parmasya

office

opisina

book shop

tindahan ng aklat

shop

tindahan

florist's

tindahan ng bulaklak

supermarket

supermarket

market

palengke

department store

department store

fishmonger's

tindahan ng isda

shopping centre

sentrong pamilihan

harbour

daungan

park

parke

bench

bangko

bridge

tulay

stairs

hagdan

underground

underground

tunnel

tunel

bus stop

hintuan ng bus

bar

bar

restaurant

restawran

postbox

kahon ng koreo

street sign

karatula sa kalsada

parking meter

metro ng paradahan

zoo

zoo

swimming pool

swimming pool

mosque

moske

farm
bukid

pollution
polusyon

graveyard
libingan

church
simbahan

playground
palaruan

temple
templo

landscape
tanawin

signpost
posteng pananda

way
daan

meadow
parang

stone
bato

hiker
hiker

tree
kahoy

river
ilog

grass
damo

flower
bulaklak

valley

lambak

hill

burol

lake

look

forest

kagubatan

desert

disyerto

volcano

bulkan

castle

kastilyo

rainbow

bahaghari

mushroom

kabute

palm tree

palmera

mosquito

lamok

fly

langaw

ant

langgam

bee

bubuyog

spider

gagamba

beetle

salagubang

frog

palaka

squirrel

ardilya

hedgehog

parkupino

hare

liyebre

owl

kuwago

bird

ibon

swan

sisne

boar

bulugan

deer

usa

moose

moose

dam

dam

wind turbine

turbina ng hangin

solar panel

solar panel

climate

klima

waiter
waiter

menu
putahe

chair
silya

soup
sopas

pizza
pizza

cutlery
kubyertos

tablecloth
mantel

starter
panimula

main course
pangunahing pagkain

dessert
panghimagas

drinks
inumin

food
pagkain

bottle
bote

fast food

fastfood

street food

pagkaing kalye

teapot

tsarera

sugar bowl

panutsa

portion

bahagi

espresso machine

espresso machine

high chair

mataas na upuan

bill

bayarin

tray

bandehado

knife

kutsilyo

fork

tinidor

spoon

kutsara

teaspoon

kutsarita

serviette

serviette

glass

baso

restaurant - restawran

plate

pinggan

soup plate

platong pansopas

saucer

platito

sauce

sawsawan

salt pot

pangkalog ng asin

pepper mill

panggiling ng paminta

vinegar

suka

oil

langis

spices

pampalasa

ketchup

ketsup

mustard

mustasa

mayonnaise

mayonnaise

special offer
espesyal na alok

customer
kustomer

dairy
produktong mantikilya

FOR

fruit
prutas

trolley
troli

butcher´s
butser

baker´s
panaderya

weigh
timbang

vegetables
mga gulay

meat
karne

frozen food
pinalamig na pagkain

cold meat

malamig na karne

tinned food

delatang pagkain

washing powder

pulbos na panlaba

sweets

matatamis

household products

mga produktong pambahay

cleaning products

mga produktong panlinis

salesperson

tindera

till

cash register

cashier

kahera

shopping list

listahan ng pinamili

opening hours

oras ng pagbubukas

wallet

pitaka

credit card

credit card

bag

bag

plastic bag

plastik bag

water

tubig

juice

juice

milk

gatas

coke

coke

wine

alak

beer

serbesa

alcohol

alak

cocoa

kakaw

tea

tsaa

coffee

kape

espresso

espresso

cappuccino

cappuccino

banana

saging

apple

mansanas

orange

kahel

melon

melon

lemon

limon

carrot

carrot

garlic

bawang

bamboo

kawayan

onion

sibuyas

mushroom

kabute

nuts

mani

noodles

noodles

spaghetti

spaghetti

rice

bigas

salad

ensalada

chips

chips

fried potatoes

pritong patatas

pizza

pizza

hamburger

hamburger

sandwich

sandwich

cutlet

piraso ng karneng walang
buto

ham

hamon

salami

salami

sausage

tsoriso

chicken

manok

roast

inihaw

fish

isda

porridge oats

mga porridge oat

muesli

muesli

cornflakes

cornflakes

flour

harina

croissant

croissant

bread roll

rolyong tinapay

bread

tinapay

toast

tostado

biscuits

biskuwit

butter

mantikilya

curd

keso

cake

keyk

egg

itlog

fried egg

pritong itlog

cheese

keso

food - pagkain

ice cream

sorbetes

sugar

asukal

honey

pulot

jam

jam

chocolate spread

tsokolateng pinapahid

curry

curry

goat

kambing

cow

baka

calf

guya

pig

baboy

piglet

biik

bull

toro

goose

gansa

duck

pato

chick

sisiw

hen

inahin

cock

katyaw

rat

daga

cat

pusa

mouse

daga

ox

kapong baka

dog

aso

doghouse

bahay ng aso

garden hose

hose sa hardin

watering can

latang pandilig

scythe

haras

plough

araro

sickle

karit

hoe

asarol

pitchfork

tuhugin

axe

palakol

wheelbarrow

karitela

trough

sabsaban

milk can

lata ng gatas

sack

sako

fence

bakod

stable

kuwadra

greenhouse

punlaan

soil

lupa

seed

buto

fertilizer

pataba

combine harvester

combine harvester

harvest

mag-ani

harvest

ani

yams

yams

wheat

trigo

soy

soya

potato

patatas

corn

mais

rapeseed

rapeseed

fruit tree

kahoy na namumunga

cassava

kamoteng kahoy

cereals

siryal

living room

salas

bathroom

palikuran

kitchen

kusina

bedroom

silid-tulugan

child's room

silid ng bata

dining room

hapag-kainan

floor

sahig

wall

pader

ceiling

kisame

cellar

bodega ng alak

sauna

sauna

balcony

balkonahe

terrace

terasa

pool

pool

lawn mower

pamputol ng damo

sheet

piraso ng papel

bedspread

kobrekama

bed

higaan

broom

walis

bucket

timba

switch

pindutan

carpet
....
karpet

curtain
....
kurtina

table
....
mesa

chair
....
silya

rocking chair
....
tumba-tumba

armchair
....
sandalan

book

aklat

blanket

kumot

decoration

dekorasyon

firewood

kahoy na panggatong

film

pelikula

hi-fi equipment

hi-fi

key

susi

newspaper

dyaryo

painting

pinta

poster

poster

radio

radyo

notepad

kuwaderno

hoover

vacuum cleaner

cactus

kaktus

candle

kandila

fridge
pridyeder

microwave oven
microwave oven

kitchen scales
timbangan sa kusina

toaster
pantusta

detergent
sabong panlaba

oven
kalan

freezer
priser

dishwasher
dishwasher

cooker

lutuan

pot

kaldero

cast-iron pot

kalderong bakal

wok / kadai

wok / kadai

pan

kawali

kettle

takore

steamer

pasingawan

baking tray

bandehado sa paghuhurno

crockery

babasagin

mug

mug

bowl

mangkok

chopsticks

sipit ng intsik

ladle

sandok

spatula

spatula

whisk

pampalis

strainer

pansala

sieve

salaan

grater

pangkayod

mortar

almires

barbecue

barbikyo

open fire

siga

chopping board

tadtaran

rolling pin

rodilyo

corkscrew

tribuson

can

lata

can opener

pambukas ng lata

pot holder

panghawak ng kaldero

sink

lababo

brush

bras

sponge

espongha

blender

blender

deep freezer

malalim na freezer

baby bottle

bote ng sanggol

tap

gripo

heating
pampainit

shower
shower

towel
tuwalya

shower curtain
kurtina sa shower

bubble bath
bubble bath

bathtub
banyera

glass
baso

washing machine
washing machine

tap
gripo

tiles
tiles

potty
arinola

sink
lababo

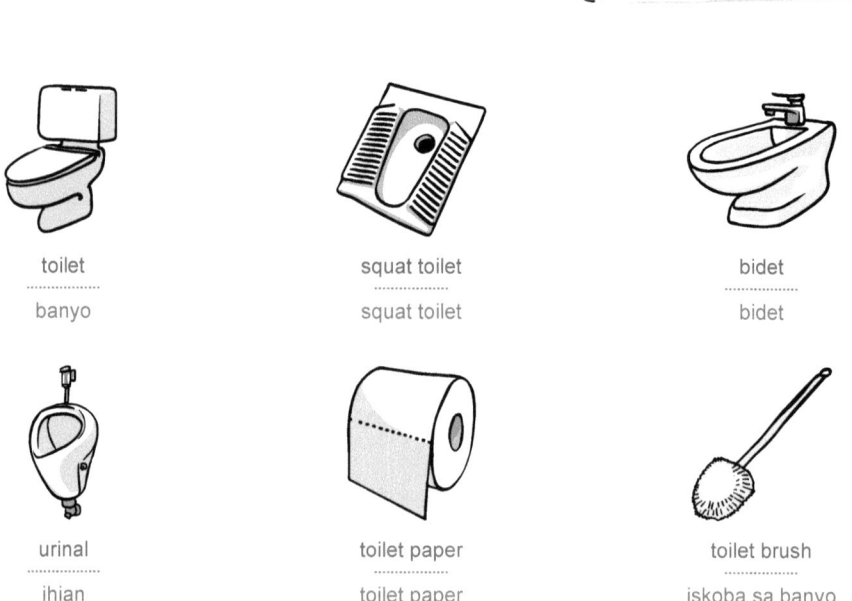

toilet
banyo

squat toilet
squat toilet

bidet
bidet

urinal
ihian

toilet paper
toilet paper

toilet brush
iskoba sa banyo

toothbrush

sipilyo

toothpaste

tutpeyst

dental floss

dental floss

wash

hugasan

handheld shower

shower na hinahawakan

douche

dutsa

basin

palanggana

back brush

bras panlikod

soap

sabon

shower gel

shower gel

shampoo

shampoo

flannel

pranela

drain

paagusan

cream

krema

deodorant

deodorant

mirror

salamin

hand mirror

salaming hinahawakan

razor

pang-ahit

shaving foam

bulang pang-ahit

aftershave

aftershave

comb

suklay

brush

brush

hair dryer

pantuyo ng buhok

hairspray

sprey sa buhok

makeup

makeup

lipstick

lipistik

nail varnish

pampakintab ng kuko

cotton wool

bulak na lana

nail scissors

panggupit ng kuko

perfume

pabango

washbag

washbag

stool

stool

weighing scale

timbangan

bathrobe

bata

rubber gloves

gomang guwantes

tampon

tampon

sanitary towel

malinis na tuwalya

chemical toilet

chemical toilet

alarm clock
alarm clock

cuddly toy
nayayakap na laruan

toy car
laruang kotse

rattle
kuliling

doll's house
bahay ng manika

present
regalo

balloon	bed	pram
lobo	higaan	pram

deck of cards	jigsaw	comic
hanay ng mga baraha	jigsaw	komiks

lego bricks
lego bricks

building blocks
blokeng laruan

action figure
action figure

babygrow
paglaki ng sanggol

frisbee
frisbee

mobile
mobile

board game
board game

dice
dice

model train set
model train set

dummy
manikin

party
salu-salo

picture book
aklat ng mga litrato

ball
bola

doll
manika

play
maglaro

sandpit

tibagan ng buhangin

swing

duyan

toys

mga laruan

video game console

video game console

tricycle

traysikel

teddy bear

teddy bear

wardrobe

aparador

clothing

pananamit

socks

medyas

stockings

stockings

tights

pampitis

scarf
bandana

belt
sinturon

umbrella
payong

t-shirt
t-shirt

trainers
sneakers

boots
bota

slippers
tsinelas

sandals
....
sandalyas

shoes
....
sapatos

rubber boots
....
botang degoma

underpants
....
salawal

bra
....
bra

vest
....
tsaleko

body

katawan

trousers

pantalon

jeans

jeans

skirt

palda

blouse

blusa

shirt

kamiseta

pullover

pullover

hoodie

panlamig

blazer

blazer

jacket

diyaket

coat

kapa

raincoat

kapote

costume

kasuotan

dress

bistida

wedding dress

damit pangkasal

suit

terno

nightgown

damit pantulog

pyjamas

padyama

sari

sari

headscarf

bandana sa ulo

turban

turban

burqa

burka

kaftan

kaftan

abaya

abaya

swimsuit

panlangoy

trunks

trunks

shorts

salawal

tracksuit

tracksuit

apron

apron

gloves

guwantes

button

butones

glasses

salamin

bracelet

pulseras

necklace

kuwintas

ring

singsing

earring

hikaw

cap

takip

coat hanger

sabitan ng kapa

hat

sombrero

tie

kurbata

zip

siper

helmet

helmet

braces

tirante

school uniform

uniporme sa paaralan

uniform

uniporme

bib

bibero

dummy

manikin

nappy

lampin

office
opisina

server
server

filing cabinet
kabinet ng file

printer
printer

monitor
monitor

paper
papel

mouse
mouse

desk
mesa

folder
polder

keyboard
keyboard

waste-paper basket
basurahan ng papel

chair
upuan

computer
kompyuter

coffee mug

tasa ng kape

calculator

calculator

internet

internet

laptop

laptop

letter

sulat

message

mensahe

mobile

mobile

network

network

photocopier

photocopier

software

software

telephone

telepono

plug socket

saksakan

fax machine

fax machine

form

anyo

document

dokumento

buy

bumili

pay

magbayad

trade

ikalakal

money

pera

dollar

dolyar

euro

euro

yen

yen

rouble

rublo

Swiss franc

swiss franc

renminbi yuan

renminbi yuan

rupee

rupee

cashpoint

cash point

bureau de change

tanggapan ng palitan ng pera

gold

ginto

silver

tanso

oil

langis

energy

enerhiya

price

presyo

contract

kontrata

tax

buwis

stock

stock

work

trabaho

employee

empleyado

employer

taga-empleyo

factory

pabrika

shop

tindahan

police officer
opisyal ng opisyal

fireman
bombero

cook
tagapagluto

doctor
doktor

pilot
piloto

gardener

hardinero

carpenter

karpentero

seamstress

mananahi

judge

hukom

chemist

kemiko

actor

aktor

bus driver

tsuper ng bus

taxi driver

tsuper ng taxi

fisherman

mangingisda

cleaning lady

tagapaglinis

roofer

tagapagkabit ng bubong

waiter

waiter

hunter

mangangaso

painter

pintor

baker

panadero

electrician

elektrisyan

builder

tagapagtayo

engineer

inhinyero

butcher

magkakarne

plumber

tubero

postman

kartero

soldier

sundalo

architect

arkitekto

cashier

kahera

florist

magtitinda ng bulaklak

hairdresser

manggugupit

conductor

konduktor

mechanic

mekaniko

captain

kapitan

dentist

dentista

scientist

siyentipiko

rabbi

rabbi

imam

imam

monk

monghe

clergyman

klero

hammer
martilyo

pliers
plais

screwdriver
distornilyador

spanner
lyabe

torch
tanglaw

digger
....
panghukay

toolbox
....
toolbox

ladder
....
hagdan

saw
....
lagari

nails
....
mga pako

drill
....
pambutas

repair

kumpunihin

shovel

pala

Damn!

Kainis!

dustpan

pandakot

paint pot

palayok ng pintura

screws

mga tornilyo

musical instruments
mga pangmusikang instrumento

loudspeaker
loud speaker

drum kit
drumset

guitar
gitara

double bass
double bass

trumpet
trumpeta

piano

piyano

violin

biyolin

bass

bass

timpani

timpani

drums

mga drum

keyboard

keyboard

saxophone

saksopon

flute

plauta

microphone

mikropono

entrance
pasukan

tiger
tigre

cage
hawla

zebra
sebra

animal feed
pakain sa hayop

panda
panda

animals
mga hayop

elephant
elepante

kangaroo
kanggaro

rhino
rhino

gorilla
gorilya

bear
oso

camel

kamelyo

ostrich

ostrich

lion

leon

monkey

unggoy

flamingo

flamingo

parrot

loro

polar bear

polar bear

penguin

penguin

shark

pating

peacock

paboreal

snake

ahas

crocodile

buwaya

zookeeper

tagapag-alaga ng zoo

seal

seal

jaguar

jaguar

zoo - zoo

pony

buriko

leopard

leopardo

hippo

hipo

giraffe

dyirap

eagle

agila

boar

bulugan

fish

isda

turtle

pagong

walrus

walrus

fox

soro

gazelle

gasel

American football
Amerikanong putbol

cycling
pamimisikleta

tennis
tennis

basketball
basketbol

swimming
paglalangoy

boxing
boksing

ice hockey
ice-hockey

football
soccer

badminton
badminton

athletics
atletiks

handball
handball

skiing
skiing

polo
polo

jump
tumalon

laugh
tumawa

hug
yakapin

walk
lumakad

sing
kumanta

dream
mangarap

pray
magdasal

kiss
halikan

write

sumulat

draw

gumuhit

show

ipakita

push

itulak

give

magbigay

take

kunin

have
magkaroon

do
gawin

be
maging

stand
tumayo

run
tumakbo

pull
hilahin

throw
itapon

fall
malaglag

lie
mahiga

wait
hintayin

carry
dalhin

sit
umupo

get dressed
magbihis

sleep
matulog

wake up
gumising

look at

tumingin

cry

umiyak

stroke

estilo

comb

magsuklay

talk

magsalita

understand

intindihin

ask

magtanong

listen

makinig

drink

uminom

eat

kumain

tidy up

linisin

love

mahal

cook

magluto

drive

magmaneho

fly

lumipad

sail

maglayag

calculate

kalkulahin

read

basahin

learn

matuto

work

trabaho

marry

pakasalan

sew

tahiin

brush teeth

magsipilyo ng ngipin

kill

patayin

smoke

manigarilyo

send

magpadala

activities - mga aktibidad

grandmother
lola

grandfather
lolo

father
ama

mother
ina

baby
sanggol

daughter
anak na babae

son
anak na lalaki

guest

panauhin

aunt

tiya

uncle

tiyo

brother

kuya

sister

ate

body

katawan

forehead
noo

eye
mata

shoulder
balikat

face
mukha

finger
daliri

chin
baba

hand
kamay

breast
suso

leg
binti

arm
bisig

baby

sanggol

man

lalaki

woman

babae

girl

batang babae

boy

batang lalaki

head

ulo

back

likod

belly

tiyan

belly button

pusod

toe

daliri ng paa

heel

takong

bone

buto

hip

balakang

knee

tuhod

elbow

siko

nose

ilong

bottom

gitna

skin

balat

cheek

pisngi

ear

tainga

lip

labi

body - katawan

mouth

bibig

tooth

ngipin

tongue

dila

brain

utak

heart

puso

muscle

kalamnan

lung

baga

liver

atay

stomach

sikmura

kidneys

mga bato

sex

pagtatalik

condom

kondom

ovum

obyum

semen

semen

pregnancy

pagbubuntis

menstruation

pagreregla

vagina

vagina

penis

ari ng lalaki

eyebrow

kilay

hair

buhok

neck

leeg

hospital
ospital

ambulance
ambulansiya

wheelchair
wheelchair

fracture
bali

doctor

doktor

emergency room

silid pang-emergency

nurse

nars

emergency

emerhensiya

unconscious

walang malay

pain

pananakit

injury

pinsala

bleeding

nagdurugo

heart attack

atake sa puso

stroke

atake serebral

allergy

alerdye

cough

ubo

fever

lagnat

flu

trangkaso

diarrhoea

pagdudumi

headache

sakit ng ulo

cancer

kanser

diabetes

diyabetis

surgeon

siruhano

scalpel

iskalpel

operation

operasyon

CT

CT

x-ray

x-ray

ultrasound

ultrasound

face mask

maskara sa mukha

disease

sakit

waiting room

silid-antayan

crutch

saklay

plaster

plaster

bandage

benda

injection

iniksyon

stethoscope

istetoskopyo

stretcher

estretser

clinical thermometer

klinikal na termometro

birth

pagsilang

overweight

labis sa timbang

hearing aid

hearing-aid

disinfectant

pang-disimpekta

infection

impeksyon

virus

bayrus

HIV / AIDS

HIV / AIDS

medicine

medisina

vaccination

bakuna

tablets

mga tableta

pill

tabletas

emergency call

emergency na tawag

blood pressure monitor

pagmamatyag sa presyon
ng dugo

ill / healthy

may sakit / malusog

Help!

Tulong!

alarm

alarma

assault

asulto

attack

atake

danger

panganib

emergency exit

labasang pang-emergency

Fire!

Sunog!

fire extinguisher

fire extinguisher

accident

aksidente

first-aid kit

kagamitan sa paunang lunas

SOS

SOS

police

pulis

Europe

Europa

North America

Hilagang Amerika

South America

Timog Amerika

Africa

Aprika

Asia

Asya

Australia

Australia

Atlantic

Atlantika

Pacific

Pasipiko

Indian Ocean

Dagat Indiano

Antarctic Ocean

Dagat Antarktika

Arctic Ocean

Dapat Arktika

North Pole

Hilagang polo

South Pole

Timog polo

Antarctica

Antartika

Earth

mundo

land

lupa

sea

dagat

island

isla

nation

bansa

state

estado

clock face

mukha ng orasan

hour hand

orasang kamay

minute hand

minutong kamay

second hand

segundong kamay

What time is it?

Anong oras na?

day

araw

time

oras

now

ngayon

digital watch

digital na relo

minute

minuto

hour

oras

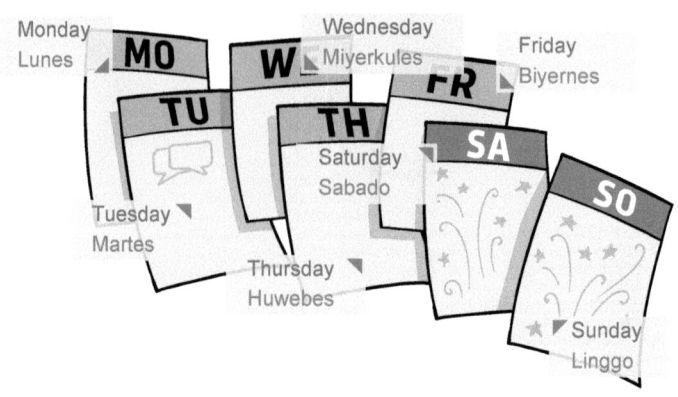

Monday / Lunes — MO
Wednesday / Miyerkules — W
Friday / Biyernes — FR
TU — Tuesday / Martes
TH
Saturday / Sabado — SA
Thursday / Huwebes
SO — Sunday / Linggo

yesterday

kahapon

today

ngayon

tomorrow

bukas

morning

umaga

noon

tanghali

evening

gabi

MO	TU	WE	TH	FR	SA	SU
1	2	3	4	5	6	7
8	9	10	11	12	13	14
15	16	17	18	19	20	21
22	23	24	25	26	27	28
29	30	31	1	2	3	4

business days

mga araw ng negosyo

MO	TU	WE	TH	FR	SA	SU
1	2	3	4	5	6	7
8	9	10	11	12	13	14
15	16	17	18	19	20	21
22	23	24	25	26	27	28
29	30	31	1	2	3	4

weekend

katapusan ng linggo

![Seasons illustration with trees showing weather conditions]

rain
ulan

spring
tagsibol

summer
tag-init

wind
hangin

autumn
taglagas

snow
niyebe

winter
taglamig

weather forecast

lagay ng panahon

thermometer

termometro

sunshine

sikat ng araw

cloud

ulap

fog

hamog

humidity

kahalumigmigan

lightning

kidlat

thunder

kulog

storm

bagyo

hail

may yelong ulan

monsoon

tag-ulan

flood

pagkain

ice

yelo

January

Enero

February

Pebrero

March

Marso

April

Abril

May

Mayo

June

Hunyo

July

Hulyo

August

Agosto

September
....
Setyembre

October
....
Oktubre

November
....
Nobyembre

December
....
Disyembre

circle
....
bilog

square
....
parisukat

rectangle
....
rektanggulo

triangle
....
tatsulok

sphere
....
pabilog

cube
....
kyub

white
....
puti

yellow
....
dilaw

orange
....
kahel

pink
....
rosas

red
....
pula

purple
....
ube

blue
....
asul

green
....
berde

brown
....
brown

grey
....
grey

black
....
itim

a lot / a little

marami / kakaunti

angry / calm

takot / kalmado

beautiful / ugly

maganda / pangit

beginning / end

simula / katapusan

big / small

malaki / maliit

bright / dark

matingkad / madilim

brother / sister

kuya / ate

clean / dirty

malinis / madumi

complete / incomplete

kumpleto / kulang

day / night

araw / gabi

dead / alive

patay / buhay

wide / narrow

malawak / makipot

edible / inedible

nakakain / hindi nakakain

evil / kind

masama / mabuti

excited / bored

nakakatuwa / nakakainip

fat / thin

mataba / payat

first / last

una / huli

friend / enemy

kaibigan / kaaway

full / empty

puno / walang laman

hard / soft

matigas / malambot

heavy / light

mabigat / magaan

hunger / thirst

gutom / uhaw

ill / healthy

may sakit / malusog

illegal / legal

ilegal / legal

intelligent / stupid

matalino / tanga

left / right

kaliwa / kanan

near / far

malapit / malayo

opposites - magkasalungat

new / used

bago /gamit na

nothing / something

wala /mayroon

old / young

matanda / bata

on / off

naka-on / naka-off

open / closed

bukas / sarado

quiet / loud

tahimik / maingay

rich / poor

mayaman / mahirap

right / wrong

tama / mali

rough / smooth

magaspang / makinis

sad / happy

malungkot / masaya

short / long

maikli / mahaba

slow / fast

mabagal / mabilis

wet / dry

basa / tuyo

warm / cool

maligamgam / malamig

war / peace

digmaan / kapayapaan

numbers

mga numero

0

zero

sero

1

one

isa

2

two

dalawa

3

three

tatlo

4

four

apat

5

five

lima

6

six

anim

7

seven

pito

8

eight

walo

9

nine

siyam

10

ten

sampu

11

eleven

labing-isa

12

twelve

labindalawa

13

thirteen

labintatlo

14

fourteen

labing-apat

15

fifteen

labinlima

16

sixteen

labing-anim

17

seventeen

labimpito

18

eighteen

labing-walo

19

nineteen

labinsiyam

20

twenty

dalawampu

100

hundred

daan

1.000

thousand

libo

1.000.000

million

milyon

languages
mga wika

English

Ingles

American English

Amerikan na Ingles

Chinese Mandarin

Tsinong Mandarin

Hindi

Hindi

Spanish

Espanyol

French

Pranses

Arabic

Arabe

Russian

Ruso

Portuguese

Portuges

Bengali

Bengali

German

Aleman

Japanese

Hapon

I

ako

you

ikaw

he / she / it

siya / siya / ito

we

kami

you

ikaw

they

sila

who?

sino?

what?

ano?

how?

paano?

where?

saan?

when?

kailangan?

name

pangalan

behind

likuran

in

saan

in front of

sa harap ng

over

itaas

on

sa

under

ilalim

beside

katabi

between

pagitan

place

lugar